Enhancing Sexuality

A Problem-Solving Approach

Therapist Guide

John P. Wincze
David H. Barlow

From The Psychological Corporation

4 5 6 7 8 9 10 11 12   B C D E

Table of Contents

About the Authors

JOHN P. WINCZE received his PhD from the University of Vermont in 1970, and has published three books and more than 50 articles and chapters, mostly in the area of sexual problems. Recent works include *Enhancing Sexuality: A Problem-Solving Approach Client Workbook* (1997); *Sexual Dysfunction: A Guide for Assessment and Treatment* (1991) coauthored by Michael Carey; "Assessment and Treatment of Atypical Sexual Behavior" (*Principles and Practice of Sex Therapy*, Leiblum and Rosen, Eds., 1989); "Marital Discord and Sexual Dysfunction Associated With a Male Partner's Sexual Addiction" (*Case Studies in Sex Therapy*, Leiblum and Rosen, Eds., 1995).

Formerly, Dr. Wincze was an associate professor of psychology at Dalhousie University, Halifax, Nova Scotia. Currently, he is a professor in the Department of Psychiatry and Human Behavior and the Department of Psychology, Brown University. He is also the Chair of the Licensing Board in Psychology for the State of Rhode Island.

DAVID H. BARLOW received his PhD from the University of Vermont in 1969, and has published 15 books and more than 200 articles and chapters, mostly in the areas of anxiety disorders, sexual problems, and clinical research methodology. Recent books include *Clinical Handbook of Psychological Disorders: A Step-by-Step Treatment Manual—Second Edition* (1993); *Anxiety and Its Disorders: The Nature and Treatment of Anxiety and Panic* (1988); *Mastery of Your Anxiety and Panic—Second Edition and Agoraphobia Supplement Therapist Guide*, coauthored by Michelle Craske (1994).

Formerly, Dr. Barlow was professor of psychiatry and psychology at Brown University. He was also Distinguished Professor in the Department of Psychology, CoDirector of the Center for Stress and Anxiety Disorders, and Director of the Phobia and Anxiety Disorders Clinic at the University of Albany, State University of New York. Currently, he is a professor of psychology, Director of Clinical Training Programs, and Director of the Center for Anxiety and Related Disorders at Boston University. Dr. Barlow is past president of the Division of Clinical Psychology of the American Psychological Association, and was awarded a merit award from the National Institute of Mental Health for "research competence and productivity that are distinctly superior." He was a member of the DSM–IV Task Force of the American Psychiatric Association. The major objective of his work for the last 15 years has been the development of new treatments for anxiety, sexual, and related disorders.

Acknowledgments

We are very grateful for all of the work that Michelle Barchi did to help put this book together. She was always uncomplaining and cheerful through the many drafts, which required her to enter and reenter the text of the book. We are also thankful to Amy Bach, who reviewed early drafts and helped shape the final version through her insightful comments. Finally, we would like to extend our thanks and acknowledge our indebtedness to John Wincze's administrative assistant, Sue Paquette, whose humor and support have helped him throughout the many years they have worked together.

Sincere thanks are in order to The Psychological Corporation, especially to Aurelio Prifitera, PhD, and Sandra Prince-Embury, PhD, for their support in bringing this product to publication. As Project Director, Dr. Prince-Embury has contributed steady support and invaluable guidance to ensure scientific precision and clinical usability of the Therapist Guide. Joanne Lenke, PhD, President of The Psychological Corporation, provided important administrative support. For much effort during the final stages of production of the *Enhancing Sexuality Therapist Guide*, hearty thanks go to John Trent, Research Assistant; Kathy Overstreet, Senior Editor; and Javier Flores, Designer.

CHAPTER 1

Introduction

This guide is intended to give mental health therapists the necessary tools to assess and treat sexual dysfunction. It will be useful for psychologists, psychiatrists, social workers, marriage and family therapists, pastoral counselors, and nurse practitioners. The information in this guide is a product of the authors' more than forty combined years of continuous research, clinical practice, and teaching in the area of sexual dysfunction.

The majority of cases referred for professional treatment of sexual dysfunction require complex and sensitive handling. This guide is intended for clinicians who are familiar with the use of the *Diagnostic and Statistical Manual of Mental Disorders—Fourth Edition* (*DSM–IV;* American Psychiatric Association, 1994) and who have clinical skills to deal with a variety of mental health problems. During the treatment of sexual dysfunction, issues of transference and countertransference often emerge. It is important, therefore, that therapists using this guide have skill in recognizing and dealing with therapy process issues.

This guide was developed from research on the development and refinement of treatment and assessment procedures (Barlow, 1972; Barlow, 1973; Barlow, 1977a, b; Caird & Wincze, 1974; Caird & Wincze, 1977; Carey, Wincze, & Meisler, 1993; Hoon, Hoon, & Wincze, 1976; Hoon, Krop, & Wincze, 1983; Hoon, Wincze, & Hoon, 1976; Hoon, Wincze, & Hoon, 1977; Malhotra, et al., 1986; Wincze, 1993; Wincze, 1995; Wincze & Barlow, 1997; Wincze & Caird, 1976; Wincze, et al., 1987; Wincze, et al., 1988; Wincze & Carey, 1991), and the basic scientific

understanding of sexual dysfunction (Abrahamson, Barlow,
& Abrahamson, 1989; Abrahamson, Barlow, Beck, Sakheim, & Kelly, 1985;
Abrahamson, Barlow, Sakheim, Beck, & Athanasiou, 1985; Balko,
et al., 1986; Barlow, 1986; Barlow, Abel, Blanchard, Bristow, & Young,
1977; Barlow, Becker, Leitenberg, & Agras, 1970; Barlow, Sakheim & Beck,
1983; Beck & Barlow, 1984a, b; Beck & Barlow, 1986a, b; Beck, Barlow
& Sakheim, 1983a, b; Beck, Barlow, Sakheim, & Abrahamson, 1987; Beck,
Sakheim & Barlow, 1983; Bruce & Barlow, 1990; Cranston-Cuebas
& Barlow, 1990; Cranston-Cuebas, Barlow, Mitchell, & Athanasiou, 1993;
Freund, Langevin & Barlow, 1974; Jones & Barlow, 1990; Lange, Brown,
Wincze, & Zwick, 1980; Lange, Wincze, Zwick, Feldman, & Hughes, 1981;
Sakheim, Barlow, Beck, & Abrahamson, 1984; Steinman, Wincze, Sakheim,
Barlow, & Mavissakalian, 1981; Wincze, Albert & Bansal, 1993; Wincze,
Hoon & Hoon, 1976; Wincze, Hoon & Hoon, 1977; Wincze, Hoon
& Hoon, 1978; Wincze, Venditti, Barlow, & Mavissakalian, 1980;
Wolchick, et al., 1980).

Our clinical experience in treating sexual dysfunction comes from
the variety of clinical settings, including a university-based clinic,
a hospital, and private practice. Finally, our experience in training clinical
psychology graduate students, psychology interns, and psychiatric
residents has helped us organize this material in a manner that is easy
for the professional therapist to use.

CHAPTER 2

Program Structure and Practical Implementation

The *Enhancing Sexuality: A Problem-Solving Approach Client Workbook* (Wincze & Barlow, 1997) is a companion product that may be used by clients involved in the therapy described in this Therapist Guide. The Therapist Guide is intended to help therapists structure a therapy program for clients seeking help for sexual dysfunction problems. This Therapist Guide is valuable for therapists whether or not clients are using the workbook, but use of the companion Client Workbook is strongly recommended. The workbook contains information and practical suggestions to help men and women improve their sexual functioning. Specifically, there is educational material, corrections of myths and misunderstandings, and basic guidelines for understanding and overcoming sexual problems. Therapy skills are needed, however, to help clients pace their progress, judge their achievement of one step before moving to the next, recognize and deal with resistance, recognize and deal with partner related issues, identify and deal with interfering nonsexual issues, and clarify issues that are poorly understood.

Who will Benefit from the Enhancing Sexuality Program

The individuals and couples who will do best with this program are those who are not overwhelmed by other nonsexual problems. Substance abuse, unstable psychotic conditions, or severe depression will most likely interfere with attempts to treat sexual dysfunction. The presence of other disorders does not necessarily interfere with this program (see Chapter 3). Your clinical judgment will help determine whether or not these other disorders are of a magnitude that will interfere with the sex therapy process.

Individuals suffering from chronic medical conditions that contribute to sexual dysfunction, such as diabetes, may also benefit from this program. Clients with medical problems will find the information useful and clarifying. In addition, they will be given guidance about how to adjust to a condition in which sexual functioning is compromised.

The full benefit of this program can best be realized by married couples or single individuals with partners. Although individuals without partners will also benefit from this program, overcoming some sexual problems is best achieved by actual experience working with a cooperative partner. The quality of a couple's relationship and the liabilities encumbering a person's sexual partner (e.g., hatred, lack of trust, lack of attraction, or medical infirmity) must be carefully weighed before embarking on treatment for sexual problems.

Frequency of Therapy Sessions

The Client Workbook is divided into 12 chapters. Chapters 2–12 are each followed by exercises, review questions, and worksheets that are designed to enhance the impact of each session. Use discretion regarding the amount of time devoted to each chapter. Page 8 provides a suggested outline for therapy sessions and the assignment of workbook chapters (if your client is using the workbook). Some chapters can be covered very quickly, but others may require more time. Usually, the therapist will meet with the client every week until all of the basic information is covered and the assessment is complete. Once actual sexual activity is being worked on, sessions are often scheduled between one and three weeks apart to allow time for homework to be completed. Sessions scheduled four or more weeks apart may cause the continuity of treatment to break down. If a couple is involved in therapy, the structure of sessions for the initial assessment follows.

Session 1

Partners are interviewed together for 10–15 minutes for the purpose of introduction. This introduction should include a review of your basic credentials and years of practice. Also, outline that the structure of therapy is dependent on the initial assessment. Finally, ask clients to give a brief summary of their problem and allow them to ask questions.

The remainder of the first session is spent with one of the two partners alone. The choice of which partner to see first is usually left up to the clients and often depends on their flexibility of schedules and availability for the next appointment. Both partners should be told that confidentiality is assured. They should be asked to report in their separate interviews whether there is information that is not to be shared. If the therapist learns information through one partner that could potentially interfere with therapy progress, this issue has to be resolved confidentially with that partner. For example, a client may disclose that he or she is having an affair and may feel that he or she is in love with this person. Such a situation is not automatically grounds for discontinuing the normal course of therapy. The therapist must remain outside of moral or personal judgment, and review all of the pros and cons of the situation with the disclosing client. After such a review, a decision should be reached about whether or not to continue therapy, and whether or not to disclose information to the uninformed partner.

Assessment of the sexual problem should include the following areas of exploration in the order they are usually addressed:

1. Basic demographics including age, composition of current household, job, length of time involved in the relationship, and educational background.

2. Brief description of the nature of the problem.

3. Medical and psychiatric history.

4. Psychosexual developmental history including childhood sexual experiences (if any), first intercourse experiences, significant messages or attitudes about sex from parents, and chronology of current or most recent sexual relationship.

5. Relationship with current partner including feelings toward current partner, and nonsexual problems with current partner (if any).

Session 2

Complete an assessment of the other partner's background, perception of the problem, and goals.

Session 3

Outline to both partners together the major issues that must be worked on, and the plan to follow the *Enhancing Sexuality* program. Discuss doing the exercises and the overall strategy.

Does Every Person Require the Entire Program

Every client will benefit from reading Chapters 1–5 and 8–12 of the Client Workbook. Because Chapters 6–7 focus on specific problems, it is only necessary for a client to concentrate on those chapters applicable to his or her problem. However, encourage the client to read all of Chapters 6–7, even if these chapters do not directly apply. These chapters will give the client a better general understanding of sexual dysfunction experienced by men and women.

Benefits of Using This Program

The information contained in this program is based on empirical research. The organization and presentation of the material is based on what has worked best in the authors' clinical experience. The manual-based structure of this program, which consists of this Therapist Guide and matching Client Workbook, has several benefits.

1. Self-paced progress.

    It is rare that therapists and clients can schedule regularly paced sessions without interruptions. The *Enhancing Sexuality* program manual allows individuals or couples to slow down or speed up sessions, or accommodate irregular personal schedules.

2. The client may refer to the Client Workbook when necessary.

For one reason or another, clients with sexual problems often participate in therapy without their partners. Partners may be supportive but too embarrassed to attend therapy sessions. In such cases, clients often convey to their nonattending partner the essence of the therapy session. Note, however, that total reliance on this indirect communication may result in inaccuracies and confusions.

Even when both partners are present at a session, there is often disagreement following a session as to the exact nature of an assignment. Some couples may do nothing rather than chance doing something wrong. Use of the Client Workbook will help avoid confusion and miscommunication.

3. Clients can read relevant material in advance.

It is helpful for clients to review material covered in each therapy session, and read relevant material in advance of their next session. This helps with continuity of treatment and often reveals problems clients may have with understanding concepts and communicating with their partners. Clients can be told to write down any areas of difficulty in their readings, and discuss those issues with the therapist on their next visit.

4. Clients can refer back to the Client Workbook after the program ends.

As an adjunct to relapse prevention training, it is helpful and comforting for clients to have the Client Workbook for reference. In most cases, review of the workbook will help the client overcome the problem without an additional therapy session. If such a review does not help the client, the problem could be more serious and require a therapeutic review in a face-to-face session.

Therapy Sessions Outline and Use of the Client Workbook

The following outline is a suggested therapy structure using the Client Workbook. This is intended as a guideline and should be flexibly adapted to each client's therapy needs.

Session #	Content of Therapy Session	Use of Client Workbook
1.	Introduction and therapy program outline. Assessment of one partner of a couple.	Review basic structure of workbook with couple. Assign Chapters 1–3.
2.	Assessment of other partner of couple.	Ask partner how reading of Chapters 1–3 is proceeding. Respond to any questions.
3.	Formulation of treatment strategy. (Chapter 3 of this book will help determine therapy pathway).	Assign Chapters 4 and 5, and either Chapter 6 or 7 if appropriate to problem. Review accomplishment of Exercises, Review, and Worksheets.
4.	Review progress for establishing priority time, and identifying factors affecting sexuality.	Review Chapters 1–5 (and 6 or 7, if assigned). Assign Chapter 8. Review Exercise, Review, and Worksheets for Chapter 5.
5.	Review progress for understanding positive and negative factors in partner relationship. Review communication.	Review Exercises, Review, and Worksheets for Chapter 8. Assign Chapter 9.

Session #	Content of Therapy Session	Use of Client Workbook
6.	Review progress to date and identify all goals established by couple. Discuss principles of sensate focus and set up agreed-upon strategy.	Review Exercises, Review, and Worksheets for Chapter 9. Assign Chapter 10.
7.	Identify all sources of sexual problems and solutions. Discuss details of sensate focus practice.	Review Exercises, Review, and Worksheets for Chapter 10. Reread Chapter 10.
8.	Review progress in sensate focus and other treatment for specific problems.	Review additional questions for Chapter 10. Assign Chapter 11.
9.	Troubleshoot any problems the couple is having with each goal and treatment procedure.	Review Exercises, Review, and Worksheets for Chapter 11. Assign Chapter 12.
10.	Discuss relapse prevention and need for further or future therapy.	Review Exercises, Review, and Worksheets for Chapter 12. Discuss use of workbook after completion of therapy.

CHAPTER 3

Assessment of Sexual Dysfunction Problems

Therapy for sexual problems works best when sexual partners are attracted to each other, are not angry with each other, and communicate effectively. Sex therapy also works best when neither partner has a comorbid Axis I or Axis II disorder, or a medical condition in need of immediate care. In many cases, however, conditions are not favorable for treating sexual problems because of the presence of a more emergent problem, or due to the presence of factors that interfere with treatment of the sexual problem. When such interfering variables are presented to the therapist, a decision has to be made regarding which problem to treat first. In some cases both problems can be treated simultaneously. This chapter will help clarify the decision process. Figure 3.1 illustrates seven possible pathways for following a comprehensive assessment.

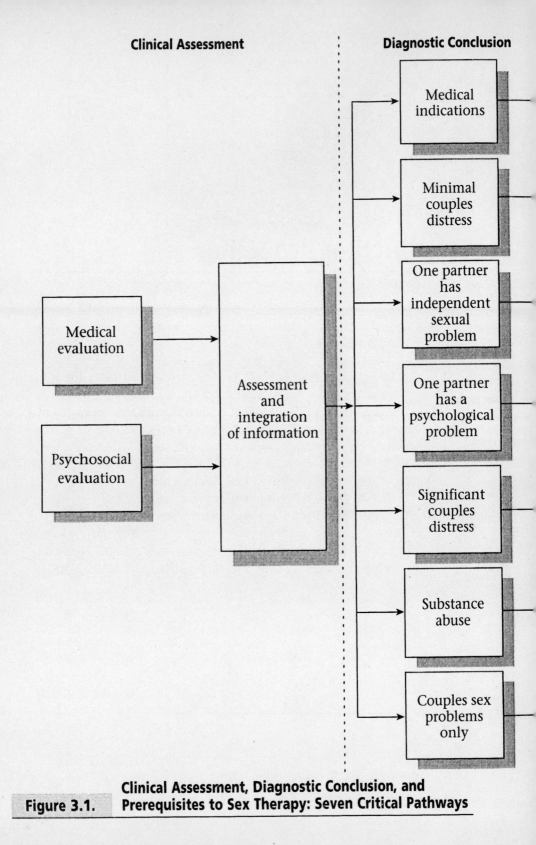

Clinical Assessment

Diagnostic Conclusion

Medical
evaluation

Psychosocial
evaluation

Assessment
and
integration
of information

Medical
indications

Minimal
couples
distress

One partner
has
independent
sexual
problem

One partner
has a
psychological
problem

Significant
couples
distress

Substance
abuse

Couples sex
problems
only

Figure 3.1.   Clinical Assessment, Diagnostic Conclusion, and
Prerequisites to Sex Therapy: Seven Critical Pathways

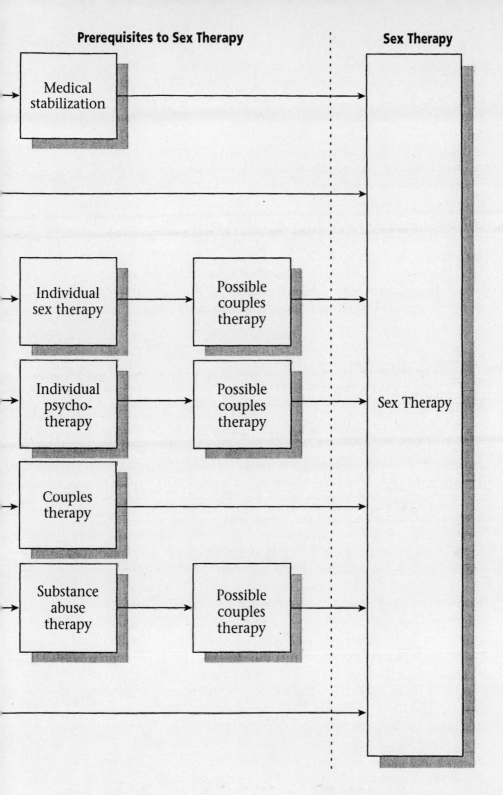

This model assumes the therapist has completed a comprehensive assessment interview and has detailed information about the nature of the sexual problem, the quality and character of a couple's relationship, the psychological profile of a client and his or her partner, and the medical history of a client and his or her partner (Wincze & Carey, 1991). This information or preliminary assessment should support a clinical determination of the primary problem and whether or not there should be treatment prerequisites to the sex therapy provided in this guide. The model outlines seven clinical pathways. The treatment pathways in Figure 3.1 will differ depending on whether or not there is a medical basis for the problem, the degree of the couples distress, the presence or absence of substance abuse, and whether one partner has a more pronounced sexual or psychological problem. Once the clinical evaluation is made, considering the above diagnostic decisions, initiate one of the following pathways.

Medical Indications

Pathway 1

If a client or his or her partner has not had a physical examination in the past year, a medical evaluation is needed. Early stages of undetected diabetes, cardiovascular disease, and neurological disease can all contribute to sexual problems (Wincze & Carey, 1991). Hormone levels for men should be obtained in cases where impotency or low desire seem to exist in all situations (i.e., partner sex, sex with a new partner, masturbation, or absence of sleep-related erections). However, if strong desire or full erections exist in at least one situation, it is less likely that the sexual problem is caused by medical factors.

If there is a strong possibility that medical factors contribute to a client's sexual problems, the options for a medical solution to the sexual problem must be explained. It is important to convey to the client that the presence of a medical factor that can cause sexual dysfunction is only an explanation for why the client is experiencing a sexual problem. The explanation does not necessitate action on the part of the client or the therapist. It is merely a starting point from which to discuss possible corrective action. A client may legitimately choose to do nothing at all about the sexual problem once he or she knows the major cause. However, the medical problem itself should be dealt with appropriately. Diabetes or cardiovascular disease, for example, must be controlled by medication or diet as fully as possible. Because these medical conditions are chronic, the client must get help adjusting to his or her disease. Some men who have such chronic diseases feel pressure to seek a medical solution for their sexual problem such as implant surgery or vasoactive injections. Some may choose to do nothing at all. The therapist's role is to be supportive, to discuss all of the options with the client, and show the pros and cons of how each option will impact him or her. It is essential to keep in mind and impress upon each client that positive conditions for sex and positive partner relations are important even when medical solutions for sex problems are exercised. Many men have been disappointed following implant surgery, or when using vasoactive injections, because they find that unsatisfactory partner relations still exist. Therapists can play a significant role in helping clients improve overall sexual satisfaction by helping them improve the conditions under which sex occurs, regardless of whether or not medical solutions to sexual problems are exercised.

Once a client's medical options are addressed, the most appropriate treatment pathway for his or her situation should be followed. If no other major issues exist, sex therapy treatment can proceed. However, if substance abuse or severe couples problems exist, these issues should be evaluated, and appropriate treatment options should be explored before sex therapy proceeds.

Minimal Couples Problems

Pathway 2

Some couples have difficulty getting along with each other although they feel positive toward and are physically attracted to each other. They may have inefficient problem-solving skills and poor communication. If the couple wishes to work toward staying together and strengthening their relationship, it is possible to address the mild relationship issues along with simultaneously working on the sexual problems. Start by directing couples to follow the instructions in the Client Workbook.

1. Prioritize time for each other.

2. Attend to the communication guidelines. Sex issues can be addressed and worked on while couples improve other aspects of their relationship. Only in cases where anger or discouragement interfere with progress should sex therapy be delayed while these issues are addressed.

Individual Psychological Problems

Pathway 3

In some cases, an individual may have such overwhelming nonsexual psychological problems that focusing on sexual problems is extremely difficult. Severe depression, post-traumatic stress disorder, acute adjustment reactions, and psychotic states are examples of psychological problems that may interfere with treatment for sexual problems. Good clinical judgment and diagnostic skills are important to determine the presence of a comorbid disorder, and in deciding how to proceed. In some cases, pharmacological intervention will stabilize a person enough to proceed, and in other cases psychotherapy must be conducted to control the psychological problem. It is not unusual for a client to overlook the impact of a nonsexual problem. The fact that a nonsexual problem preceded the sexual problem, does not mean that it isn't contributing to the sexual problem. For example, depression symptoms may have been overridden by the newness of a sexual relationship and only when a couple became more familiar with each other over time might the depression interfere with sex. If this is confusing to a client, explain how the depression is interfering with sex now, and why it may require specific treatment. Once the comorbid psychological problem has been addressed and progress has been noted, the sexual problem can be addressed, in most cases, without interference.

Individual Sexual Problems

Pathway 4

In general, it is best to approach the treatment of sexual problems as a "couple's" problem (if a partner exists). Following the intake assessment, both partners should usually be seen together, in order to reduce blame and facilitate communication. However, in some cases, an individual may have brought into a relationship such unique or overwhelming sexual issues that it is important to work with the client without his or her partner. For example, a male client may have severe paraphiliac problems that interfere with a couple's sexual relations. As defined in DSM–IV, a paraphiliac problem is one in which there are "recurrent intense sexually arousing fantasies, sexual urges, or behavior generally involving 1) nonhuman objects, 2) the suffering or humiliation of oneself or one's partner, or 3) children or other nonconsenting persons." This condition must be present over a period of at least 6 months and involve distress or impairment in social, occupational, or other important areas of functioning. It may be important for the therapist to work alone with the male partner in order to understand the intensity and importance of the paraphiliac behavior. Once this is learned, a decision must be made to either control the paraphiliac behavior or integrate it in an acceptable manner into the sexual relations of the couple.

Another example of a specifically individual sexual problem might be that of a woman who has a history of childhood sexual abuse. Her fear or aversion to sex may have to be dealt with individually to address anger, shame, or guilt issues that are often present. Once these issues are satisfactorily put into perspective, her partner should be included to help him or her understand the effects that the abuse has had.

Severe Couples Problems

Pathway 5

Couples often enter sex therapy with very severe relationship problems that predate their sexual problems. It is common for couples to focus on their sexual problem although relationship problems contribute to the sexual problem. It is sometimes easier for couples to identify sexual dysfunction as "wrong" and a source of "blame" than to identify complex communication or problem-solving deficiencies.

When unresolved anger or other negative feelings have existed for 6 months or more, these contributing factors must be addressed before sexual issues. Most couples readily agree with the strategy to delay addressing the sexual problems and initially address the couples issues. Even when couples understand the reasons for this, it is important to periodically review with them the rationale for the strategy, and the progress and goals obtained.

Once couples have resolved relationship problems and positive feelings exist, therapy may proceed to directly addressing sexual difficulties. Because many strategies helpful in overcoming relationship problems are also common to solving sexual problems, couples can use the Client Workbook. Specifically, couples should review the sections on setting aside quality time and practicing communication.

Substance Abuse or Dependence

Pathway 6

When substance abuse or dependence is suspected in an individual seeking therapy, or in either partner of a couple, the substance problem must be accurately assessed and treated first. We have never found it productive to delay treatment for substance problems, or to attempt to deal with these problems along with sexual problems. As a general rule, we require an individual to be "clean" for a minimum of three months before addressing sexual problems. The three-month period allows individuals to adjust to not abusing substances, and to filling their time with more constructive activities. It is also a time for individuals to adjust to communicating and solving problems without drugs or alcohol. This is often a stressful time and therefore a time when great energy has to be placed on staying sober.

During this time, individuals are likely to encounter an increase in sexual difficulties. This is usually due to an awareness and self-consciousness about sexual matters. There may also be anger issues that have to be worked through that may keep the other partner at a distance and away from intimacy. In our judgment, the three-month sobriety period demonstrates the seriousness and steadfastness of a person's efforts, and allows for time to establish an environment conducive to working on sexual problems.

When at all possible, we advise individuals to postpone sexual activity during the initial three months of sobriety. Often, when an individual discontinues substance use, sexual difficulties are exacerbated. Unresolved problems, anger, racing thoughts, and relationship issues come to the surface and are faced for the first time. Many therapists will find, at this point, that the unresolved relationship problems or individual psychological problems exposed by the abstinence period are severe enough to delay sex therapy until these other issues are dealt with. Individuals and couples should be made aware of this possibility, and be advised to approach sexual relations with a primary focus on establishing the right conditions for "intimacy." De-emphasize performance during the initial stages of abstinence. Therefore, when a client has a substance problem and follows your advice to seek help for this, inform him or her of possible difficulties during the initial stages of abstinence, and prepare him or her with a strategy to prevent exacerbating the sexual problems. Once abstinence has been in place for at least three months, sexual problems can be dealt with more directly.

When therapy proceeds, it should be pointed out that preoccupation with these problems during the initial stages of abstinence can directly interfere with sexual functioning.

No Apparent Complicating Problems—Initiate Sex Therapy

Pathway 7

When your assessment reveals a situation with no complicating medical, interpersonal, psychological, or substance abuse problems, sex therapy can begin. Such cases generally progress satisfactorily. Use the Client Workbook to facilitate the process. It offers a structural guide for clients and therapists during the therapy sessions. The client can refer to the workbook to bridge the time between sessions (especially if there are unexpected delays between regularly scheduled sessions), and thereby stay on track.

CHAPTER 4

Therapy Outline: Building Blocks to Understand and Assess Sexual Problems
(Client Workbook Chapters 1–3)

There are three main components to the *Enhancing Sexuality* program. The first component focuses on understanding the importance of accurate sexual information and positive sexual attitudes. It helps clear up sexual myths and misunderstandings, which is important to establish the best conditions for a therapeutic process. The second component is an accurate assessment to help an individual or couple pinpoint the positive and negative factors that affect sexual functioning. The third component works through the actual therapeutic process and builds relapse prevention.

Chapters 4 and 5 help the therapist guide the client through the first two components of the program. These two components are covered in Chapters 1–5 of the Client Workbook. These chapters should be completed by a client or couple during the first three therapy sessions. The exercise found at the end of Chapter 2, in which couples set aside time for each other to discuss sexual beliefs, is fundamental for subsequent sessions.

This and remaining sections of the Therapist Guide will follow a similar structure. They will describe the principles underlying a particular treatment procedure included in the lesson, describe the main concepts conveyed to an individual or couple in the lesson, and summarize information point by point. There are also case examples that reflect typical types of questions asked in each lesson, with examples of therapist responses. Finally, there is a description of unusual or problematic client responses.

Principles Underlying Treatment

Two underlying treatment principles to help clients through the first two components are that sexual problems are extremely common in men and women, and that sexual problems do not make a person weak, abnormal, or mentally ill. It shows that men and women can enhance their sexuality by overcoming their sexual problems or learning alternate ways of pleasure.

Main Concepts Conveyed to Client

First, because sexual information is usually not taught in an open and comprehensive way, men and women are often subject to sexual misunderstandings that can interfere with sexual functioning. Clients learn that accurate sexual information can sometimes correct sexual difficulties and remove blame. Second, men and women often react differently to their own sexual problems and to their partner's. It is usually necessary to understand these differences in order to overcome sexual problems. Third, sexual attitudes and behavior are largely influenced by a person's learning history. Observed and experienced sexual information in childhood and adolescence strongly influences adult sexuality. Understanding this concept helps remove blame and the notion that one partner is right or wrong. Finally, although medical factors can affect sexual functioning, it is usually necessary to conceptualize sexual problems as having possible contributions from medical and nonmedical (e.g., psychological, or interpersonal) factors to understand the full picture.

Summary of Information

Summary of Information for the first component of the Client Workbook includes discussion of misunderstandings, myths, attitudes, and therapy conditions.

- Definition of sexual problems, including general description and common types experienced by men and women.

- General description of causes of sexual problems, including medical, psychological, and situational factors.

- Description of how men's and women's reactions to their sexual problem can cause further problems, and how sexual myths and misunderstandings cause problems.

- Description of how sexual patterns (e.g., behavior, or attractions) and attitudes develop; helps clients remove blame, and helps them understand that everyone is a product of their learning history.

The information in the second component of the Client Workbook (Chapters 4–5) pinpoint positive and negative factors that affect sexual functioning. These chapters include the following:

- Description of medical factors affecting sexual functioning, including diseases, medications, drugs, and alcohol.

- Review of most common biological (medical), psychological, and interpersonal factors affecting sexual functioning.

- Diagram to help clients identify all positive and negative factors affecting their sexual functioning.

Case Example

Clients entering sex therapy are often embarrassed and fearful that their problem is unique and makes them abnormal. The therapist must help the client feel comfortable by stressing how common sexual problems are, and that sexual problems are not signs of serious mental illness. An initial therapy session example follows. Use this dialog key for all Case Examples—T=Therapist, C=Client, P=Client's partner (i.e., spouse or lover).

 T: Hi, I am Dr. _____. I want to begin by helping you understand what I'll be doing today. First of all, I want you to know that it is difficult for most people to discuss sexual issues. Sexual problems, however, are very, very common. Sometimes the cause of such problems is medical, and sometimes the cause is just due to a person's situation. What I will be doing today is reviewing both medical and nonmedical factors and seeing which factors apply to you.

(At this point, explain to the couple that each will be interviewed alone on separate occasions.)

T: By the end of the assessment I will be able to outline for you what the best course of treatment is for your problem. Do you have any questions?

C: How many sessions will this take? I know you probably can't tell me exactly, but what is the usual time?

T: You are right. I cannot give you an exact number of sessions, although the program is designed for 10 sessions. There are some people who move through the program more quickly, and in some cases it is necessary to deal with other problems before working directly on sexual problems.

C: What do you mean by other problems?

T: Sometimes I work with people who are in a very stressful relationship. It is important that a person feels comfortable and positive toward his or her partner before working on sexual problems. Issues of anger and poor communication have to be worked on first. Other people I deal with have drinking or drug problems that need to be worked on first.

C: Oh, I see. So what do you want to know?

T: Well, please start by telling me about your current living situation. Who is living in your household?

(Generally, the therapist will proceed by obtaining basic background information before asking about the specific details of the sexual problem or psychosexual history.)

Atypical and Problematic Responses

When a client searches for the cause of a sexual problem, he or she may rigidly adhere to a single explanation. This is especially true of men who are convinced that their problem is a result of medical factors. There is little comfort for the client, however, in telling such a man that he is perfectly healthy and that his problem is not medical. The hope is that the problem is medical (and therefore not their fault), and that it can be corrected with a pill or some other simple medical procedure.

In such cases, it is important for the therapist to point out that it is good news that there are no medical factors involved. All men are susceptible to interference in their sexual responding. It does not make them unusual or mean they have a psychological problem. It is also important to point out that medical factors affect a man in *all* situations and not just with his sexual partner. If a sexual response (arousal, erection, orgasm) can occur during masturbation, with another partner, or during sleep, a medical explanation is unlikely and certainly not the only explanation.

CHAPTER 5

Problems with Desire and Arousal

Chapters 4 and 5 in the Client Workbook are important for all clients because they help clearly identify positive and negative factors that may be affecting sexual functioning and arousal. Thus, although these chapters address specific problems, the content is applicable to other disorders as well. All clients, regardless of their problem, should read Chapters 4 and 5.

Principles Underlying Treatment

The principle conveyed in this lesson is that sexual encounters provide varied experiences. Each sexual experience is effected by the balance between positive and negative factors.

Main Concepts Conveyed to Client

The main concept conveyed to clients is that sex is not an automatic biological function. It is effected by many factors, especially those relating to a partner. Many clients we have treated have been operating under very adverse sexual conditions, yet the clients have been baffled as to why they have been experiencing sexual problems. Some clients experience a great deal of stress in their lives, or they attempt sex under nonerotic conditions, yet have the full expectations that sex should occur unaffected. The therapist must emphasize that all men and women require "favorable" conditions for sex to occur successfully. The client's sexual problems under adverse conditions are common to anyone exposed to "unfavorable" conditions. "Unfavorable" conditions may be biological, psychological, or interpersonal. Such conditions can adversely affect sexual desire as well as sexual arousal in men and women. Sexual desire problems for men and women refer to a lack of lust, passion, or desire. DSM–IV classifies such problems as "Hypoactive Sexual Desire Disorder," and includes symptoms of persistent absence of sexual fantasies and desire for sexual activity. Furthermore, these occurrences are stressful or cause interpersonal difficulty.

Sexual arousal problems relate to actual physiological function. DSM–IV classifies such problems as "Female Arousal Disorder" and "Male Erectile Disorder." Symptoms include a lack of female lubrication response and a lack of male erection response. For both men and women, the symptoms also include personal or interpersonal distress.

Summary of Information

The information below applies to both sexual desire and sexual arousal problems.

- A person's sexual functioning at any given moment is effected by the presence or absence of positive and negative biological, psychological, and interpersonal factors. It is important to help your clients identify positive and negative factors that may be currently operating and affecting their sexual functioning.

- Interfering thoughts affect men more than women during sexual activity. Such thoughts are often performance oriented, and may trigger loss of erection and inhibit intercourse. The loss of erection is observable, and therefore men feel more pressure.

- A sexual partner's attitude and enthusiasm for sex are extremely important, yet they are often overlooked as factors that facilitate arousal. The therapist has to identify these factors as strengths the client can capitalize on rather than as sources of blame.

- The reasons why individuals engage in sex may change from one sexual encounter to another. Clients should understand this to bring expectations in line with reality. Sexual encounters don't always have to be physically exciting, but may still be meaningful because of the psychological satisfaction.

- Age contributes to sexual changes for men and women and it is important to understand that these changes are normal. Such changes do not signal an end to sex, but rather an adjustment that must be accepted to keep sex running smoothly.

Case Example

Client's entering sex therapy often look for a single explanation to their sexual problem. Clients often overlook obvious factors such as negative feelings toward one's partner. It is easier, and perhaps more acceptable, to identify a single medical problem than to face the complexity and unknown characteristic of a psychological or interpersonal problem as the source of sexual dysfunction.

T: Please tell me when you first started to experience erection problems.

C: It all started about a year before my wife and I decided to get a divorce.

T: You have been married for about 15 years. When did you and your wife start having trouble getting along?

C: When I think about it, it has been the last five years that we haven't gotten along. It became very nasty and we fought a lot. It seems like we were always angry at each other.

T: Did you and your wife attempt sex during the last year of your marriage?

C: Yes, we would try every once in a while. When I tried though, I would lose my erection and she would get furious. She would say, "Why do you bother to get me involved in sex when you can't follow through?" I felt awful and got angry and depressed.

T: Since your divorce, have you been with other women?

C: Yes. And this is what I can't understand. I met a very attractive woman and on the third date I tried to have sex, but failed. I thought that my wife was the problem, but now I know it is my fault.

T: How did this new woman react when you lost your erection?

C: Well, at first she seemed to understand, but soon she started to say things like it wasn't her job to arouse me, and that she never had this problem with other men.

T: What do you think is causing your problem?

C: I don't know, but there must be something wrong with my body, because it happened with two different women. The new woman I was with was attractive and wanted sex, but I couldn't perform. I wanted to, but it just didn't work.

T: Are there any other times that you do experience erections? It is normal for men to experience erections when they sleep, or when they wake up in the morning. It is also normal for men to experience erections during masturbation, or when looking at sexually explicit pictures. What is your experience?

C: Well, I get full erections at those times, but not when I need it. Is there a pill you can give me to help with the erections? I heard that some men take pills to give them erections. Are there vitamins or stimulants of some sort?

T: It is a very positive sign that you can get erections at night or when looking at sexually explicit pictures. This means that your body is functioning normally. There are many different factors that can interfere with a man's sexual functioning, and what we have to do is figure out what is affecting your situation. There also may be different reasons at different times, so that factors that affected you with your wife may be different than the factors that affected you with your girlfriend.

There are no vitamins that can help you with erections, but in certain cases some medications may be helpful. First, however, let's look at some possible factors that may have affected your sexual response with your wife and with your girlfriend. Let's start by reviewing the situation with your wife. You said you were very angry at your wife. Did you really feel like having sex when you were angry?

Atypical or Problematic Responses

It is often difficult for clients to identify certain current factors as problematic when these same factors did not previously inhibit sex. For example, a man who consumes 3 or 4 drinks of hard liquor a night may disconnect the liquor as a contributor to his impotency, because he always drank as much in the past and did not experience sexual problems. The balancing scale in Figure 5.1 (also included on page 41 of the Client Workbook) may help a client conceptualize why the liquor could be a factor now, and was not a factor in the past. The therapist can help the client identify positive facilitating and negative inhibiting factors in the past and present.

Usually, factors such as age, stress level, physical condition, and partner relationship are relevant for such a discussion. The relevant point of your discussion should be that moderate to heavy drinking of alcohol is a negative factor because of its physiological inhibiting properties. The importance of this inhibition may only manifest itself when other negative factors are present, or when positive factors are absent.

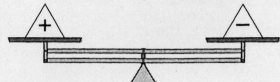

Psychological Factors	Good emotional health	Depression or PTSD
	Attraction toward partner	Lack of partner attraction
	Positive attitude toward partner	Negative attitude toward partner
	Positive sex attitude	Negative attitude toward sex
	Focus on pleasure	Focus on performance
	Newness	Routine, habit
	Good self-esteem	Poor self-esteem
	Comfortable environment for sex	Uncomfortable environment for sex
	Flexible attitude toward sex	Rigid, narrow attitude toward sex
Physical Factors	No smoking	Smoking
	No excess alcohol	Too much alcohol
	No medications that effect sex	Antihypertensive medication (heart)/drugs
	Good physical health	Poor physical health
	Regular, appropriate exercise	Heart and blood-flow problems
	Good nutrition	Diabetes
	Successful Sexual Functioning	**Dysfunctional Sexual Functioning**

Figure 5.1.   **Positive and Negative Factors That Affect Sexual Functioning**

CHAPTER 6

Problems with Ejaculation and Orgasm

Clients should understand at this point that their sexual problem
is a result of the presence of various inhibiting factors or the absence
of sufficient facilitating factors. Several factors such as age, arousal,
and time since last orgasm affect speed of ejaculation in men. For men
or women who are experiencing delayed or absent orgasm, this chapter
will explore medical factors and consider the possibility of low desire, lack
of erotic stimulation, and lack of sexual skills as concomitant problems.

Men and women vary widely in the type and intensity of stimulation
that triggers orgasm (DSM–IV). The intensity and pleasure of orgasm
also varies widely within each individual depending on numerous
facilitating or inhibiting factors, such as length of the relationship.
The therapist should explain all of these dimensions to clients reporting
orgasm problems, so clients can formulate realistic expectations regarding
their orgasmic experience.

Even with realistic expectations and sufficient erotic stimulation, there
are still many men and women who do not achieve orgasm. The etiology
of orgasmic dysfunction in such cases may be related to insecure
or stressful partner relations. In these cases, therapy should focus
on couples issues first, then on sexual dysfunction issues. Once couples
have achieved a sufficient level of comfort and compatibility in their
relationship, orgasmic problems can be focused on. In addition
to the guidelines that follow and the sensate focus strategy from
Chapter 10, open-minded couples may derive a great deal of pleasure

and orgasmic success with the use of a vibrator. Few individuals think of using a vibrator, yet vibratory stimulation has been shown to be a reliable elicitor of arousal and orgasm for both women and men (Turner & Rubinson, 1993).

Another pleasure and orgasm enhancer is lubricant jelly. Suggesting the use of a vibrator or lubricant should be carefully approached so as not to offend or frighten the client. The therapist should present such suggestions as "options that some clients have found helpful." Clients who are interested in exploring such options may need guidance as to where to purchase vibrators (usually department stores or large chain drug stores) or lubricant jelly (over the counter at drug stores) and may need instructions on use. Instruct clients that there is no right or wrong use, but that direct stimulation with a vibrator on the clitoris or glans may be too intense and uncomfortable. Clients should be encouraged to explore these options over a number of occasions, and not give up after one try. There is some skill acquisition involved.

Premorbid sexual aversion may be the cause of orgasmic problems. This is related to a negative sexual history that includes fear or an aversion to sex. These issues must be addressed and worked through in individual therapy before proceeding with the above suggestions for enhancing orgasm.

Some people purposely hold back from letting themselves orgasm because of either fear of fainting, fear that the orgasm will make them look foolish, or fear that the orgasm will lead to an out of control response. In such cases, individuals can benefit from discussion about the orgasmic experience as a normal, healthy response. Addressing myths or misunderstandings about orgasm, and reviewing the physiology of orgasm, may be helpful.

Principles Underlying Treatment

The important therapeutic principle in treating ejaculation or orgasmic problems is to avoid increasing the pressure to perform. If a therapist focuses on ejaculation or orgasm, and teaches skills to improve them, therapy may fail because it feeds into performance anxiety. A more successful approach is to focus on general pleasure and enjoyment of sexual encounters. Ejaculation and orgasm should be viewed as part of a whole sexual experience. The psychological value, pleasure, and meaning should be emphasized along with sensual pleasure. By emphasizing psychological satisfaction along with more general sensual pleasure, there is less likelihood that a client will feel increased performance anxiety created by the therapist.

Therapists may unwittingly put performance pressure on their clients with orgasmic problems by directly asking a client if orgasm was experienced during the practice. Remember, the goal is increasing pleasure, and the therapist should ask about pleasure. Clients will spontaneously report if orgasm was experienced.

Main Concepts Conveyed to Client

One concept to convey to clients is that ejaculation and orgasm are only part of the total pleasure possible from a sexual exchange. The defining criteria of sexual success should not be ejaculation or orgasm alone. By helping a client focus on all aspects of a total sexual experience, pressure is removed from the focus on ejaculation and orgasm.

A related concept is that, in most cases, orgasms do not have to occur at a specific interval of time or in both partners simultaneously for sex to be pleasurable or "successful." The therapist should emphasize to clients that orgasms may occur before or after one's partner orgasms, or that orgasms may not occur at all on some occasions, but that sex can still be pleasurable and satisfying. Such instructions tend to increase the overall likelihood of sexual pleasure and remove the focus from sexual performance.

Summary of Information

■ There are several factors such as age (younger men tend to ejaculate more quickly), amount of arousal, and time since last orgasm that affect speed of ejaculation in men. However, ejaculation is difficult for most men to control, and there may be very little that men can do to control their ejaculation. The therapy should help a man and his partner enjoy sexual pleasure, rather than focus on performance. If a therapist emphasizes control of ejaculation, he or she may be reinforcing the performance emphasis to the client.

- Orgasms for men and women can vary in intensity. It is important for the therapist to challenge misunderstandings that normal orgasms are intense. Familiarity, as in the case of long-term partnerships, often reduces intensity of the orgasmic experience.

- Men and women differ in several ways concerning the experience of orgasm. Women, in general, are less orgasmic than men, but are more capable of multiple orgasms (Masters, Johnson, & Kolodony, 1992).

Case Example

T: You stated that your problem is premature ejaculation. I deal with a lot of men who also state they are experiencing premature ejaculation, but I've found out that people's definition of this problem varies quite a bit. Some men I see consider it premature ejaculation because they consistently ejaculate before they enter their partner. Other men feel that they are premature if they ejaculate before 15 minutes. What is your definition? What has been your experience with ejaculation?

C: Well, I don't ejaculate before intercourse, but I only last a minute or two.

T: And what happens when you ejaculate? How do you feel, and how do you react?

C: I get very angry, and I usually apologize to my wife.

P: He gets so upset that he completely ruins the mood. I'm getting to the point that I don't even want sex because we both get so upset. He makes me upset because he is upset. I tell him it doesn't matter, but he doesn't listen.

T: I think part of the problem is the way you are reacting. Sex should be pleasurable and something

that is enjoyed. It shouldn't be a performance.
What I will try to do in therapy is help you learn
to enjoy your sex experience and not fear it.

Tell me what your usual sexual experience is like?
How long do you usually last during sexual
relations?

C: I think it's only about a minute or so. Sometimes
even less.

T: What have you done to try to control it?

C: I've tried thinking of other things like work
or sports, but that doesn't work.

P: Also, he won't let me touch him. We hardly have
any foreplay because he's afraid he'll ejaculate.
I just lay there. I don't know what to do
anymore. It's awful. I sometimes cry afterwards.

T: How long do you think sex should last?

C: I don't know, but certainly longer than I can now.
I know that guys may exaggerate and say they
can last for 30 minutes or more, but my friend says
he lasts 15 minutes. I believe him.

T: Well, your friend may be telling the truth,
but actually most men last about 2–8 minutes.
The most important point is that you and your
partner enjoy what you are doing. By focusing
everything on how long you last, you have
made sex tense and unpleasant. It is important
for both of you to work toward enjoying sex
and not worry about performing. The first thing
you must do is forget about how long you last,
and enjoy what you are doing. Many couples
who experience quick ejaculation will approach
sex with different strategies to work around this
behavior. For example, some couples will bring
the female partner to orgasm before or after
intercourse by hand stimulation or oral sex. Also,

it is important to not get angry or frustrated
when you ejaculate. Rather, enjoy the experience.
After you ejaculate, continue with intercourse.
Many men can maintain their erection
for a minute or two after ejaculation, and this
can help couples enjoy sex more. Why
do you think you ejaculate quickly?

 I don't know. I just thought that I had weak
nerves or something. I tried to tell her I couldn't
control it, but she didn't believe me.

 Well, I just think you are out for yourself. You're
always out with your buddies, you don't talk
about our problems, and it just seems like
you have no time for me.

T: It sounds like some other issues might be affecting
how you feel about each other.

Clinical Comment

The exchange with this couple is typical. It illustrates the usual
combination of misunderstandings, maladaptive approaches, and general
relationship problems. Premature ejaculation complaints rarely come from
couples who get along well and have an otherwise satisfactory sexual
relationship. Unless the problem is extreme, most couples who
do get along well can work around premature ejaculation.

Atypical or Problematic Responses

Treatment of premature ejaculation is more difficult in the single
male who is not working with a cooperative, trusting partner. Working
with a partner provides a greater opportunity for a common understanding
and a common set of sexual goals. A single male without a steady
partner has to deal with unpredictable partner responses. Also, because
the single male must be more concerned about sexually transmitted
diseases and unwanted pregnancy, he cannot afford mistakes with
condom misuse. Consequently, he must withdraw immediately after
ejaculation so that his condom won't fall off. Thus, attention is focused
on ejaculation.

The emphasis in treating a single male with premature ejaculation is to focus on partner selection and general sexual skills. The man should be encouraged to select a partner who is nonjudgmental, easy to talk to, and sexually flexible. A man who selects a judgmental and rigid person is likely to encounter much more pressure and disappointment. With the "right" partner, the man should be able to focus on more general pleasure, and sexually please his partner in a variety of ways.

CHAPTER 7

Problems with Pain and Discomfort During Sexual Penetration

A medical etiology should always be considered whenever pain or discomfort are present during penetration. In cases where the pain is present with one partner but not with other partners, a medical explanation is less likely. Partner-specific pain suggests partner-specific problems, and not medical problems.

Principles Underlying Treatment

Dyspareunia is defined as a "recurrent or persistent genital pain associated with sexual intercourse in either a male or a female" (DSM–IV, p. 513). This disturbance causes marked distress or interpersonal difficulty. Vaginismus is specific to females who experience involuntary perennial muscle spasms associated with attempts at any vaginal insertion (e.g., penis, finger, tampon).

Therapy for dyspareunia or vaginismus must help the client feel normal, and must reassure the client that therapy will not force an individual to participate in sex against his or her will. Therapy will not include any unexpected surprises and will be within the control of the client. The client must be reassured that the therapeutic process is without pressure, and that the therapist is trustworthy.

Main Concept Conveyed to Client

The main concept to convey to clients is that any behavior can be broken down into smaller, more gradual components. Clients are used to conceptualizing intercourse as all or none. The therapist can help structure a gradual approach to penetration. For example, the approach to penetration can begin with the client privately practicing touching her labia. Steps toward realization of penetration may include brief, partial penetration using one finger, then insertion of two fingers for longer periods of time.

Summary of Information

- Even after pain and discomfort are treated medically, there may be a need to use a gradual behavioral approach to address residual anxiety related to sexual relations. Explore anticipatory pain in such clients.

- Explore how the client's pain and discomfort have possibly affected his or her partner. There is often concern about pain even after successful treatment. A partner may be reluctant to approach sex because of a fear of causing further pain. This is often a problem in couples with poor communication, where pain may have been endured silently. The need for open communication must be addressed in such couples.

Case Example

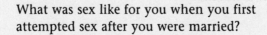

T: Have you always experienced pain during sexual intercourse, or have there been times in the past when sex has been comfortable for you?

C: I never had sex with anyone before marriage, and my husband and I both agreed to hold off on sex until we got married.

T: What was sex like for you when you first attempted sex after you were married?

C: Our honeymoon was awful. I felt like my husband was attacking me and I started crying. I kept feeling like he was going to hurt me if he penetrated me. We tried more than once but it never worked out. He became very angry and the whole honeymoon was spoiled. The hardest part was that, after our honeymoon, people would ask us how it was and everyone assumed we had great sex. It really hurt to lie to people.

T: Why did you feel that sex was going to hurt?

C: I don't know. I just remember hearing that sex could hurt. My mother never talked to me at all about sex, but she warned me not to get pregnant. I know my family would have disowned me if I got pregnant before marriage.

T: Were you ever comfortable with inserting your finger or a tampon in your vagina?

C: Oh, never! I don't even look at myself down there. I know that some women do that, but I feel I would hurt myself if I inserted anything. I believe I am built differently than other women, and inserting something might hurt.

T: Has a doctor ever examined you and told you that you were built differently?

C: No. I haven't been to a doctor for a few years, and the last time I went to a doctor I wouldn't let him examine me down there.

T: How would you feel about going to a doctor now?

C: I would be very nervous, but I know it is necessary.

Clinical Comment

It is very important for women like this client to have a thorough medical examination. A current medical examination can reassure her that she is physically normal, or provide specific information regarding a physical cause for pain associated with penetration. In this client's case, there are also nonmedical reasons for her pain. She is very uncomfortable with her body in general, and she is uncomfortable about sex. It is extremely important to deal with cognitive issues associated with pain or even the anticipation of pain. Dealing with cognitive issues will help facilitate a behavioral approach to a more satisfying sexual experience, possibly through a gradual insertion approach to intercourse.

In many cases, sexual problems are linked specifically to problems with body image. In this case, the client's poor body image was related to negative messages about sex from her mother, and also related to a severe case of acne she had as a teenager. Acne and weight problems in teen years may result in an insecurity about one's appearance. This may extend even into adulthood, long after the teenage acne or weight problems have disappeared. In such cases, the therapist can help work with the client to identify positive body traits and challenge automatic negative thinking about body image. Practice in looking at oneself in the mirror may also help desensitize the client to poor body image.

Body image problems may also be more severe signs of psychopathology in the form of body dysmorphic disorder. In such cases, long-term psychotherapy may be necessary for any progress to occur.

Women who experience pain or discomfort during sex may also avoid going to medical doctors. The fear of a medical examination of one's genitals may be greater than the fear of a medical disease. In such cases, it is helpful to identify a physician or nurse practitioner who is sensitive to this problem, and who can help the woman desensitize herself to the fear, using a gradual, repeated approach to medical examination.

Atypical or Problematic Responses

For the treatment of most sexual problems, a cooperative and understanding partner greatly facilitates progress. In the treatment of vaginismus or dyspareunia, the partner's support and cooperation are especially important.

In some cases, a partner can interfere with progress. We have had some cases in which the male partner had strong beliefs that intercourse was the only acceptable sexual practice. Consequently, a gradual approach to intercourse or sexual interactions without intercourse were not acceptable. Because of very restricted beliefs by a male partner, there is more pressure on the female and less chance for desensitization to occur. Trust and control are very important to the female experiencing dyspareunia or vaginismus. When the male's sexual beliefs supersede the female partner's wishes, the female's sense of control and trust is undermined, making successful treatment extremely difficult.

In a situation where a couple's beliefs are in conflict and may interfere with treatment, the therapist should explore every possibility of compromise with the couple. The differences in beliefs should be addressed as objectively as possible, so that neither partner feels blamed or at fault for their beliefs. By openly discussing the issue in an objective fashion, the partners are presented with the limitations or obstacles they are facing. Some couples will accept a change in their beliefs as a "temporary" change to solve a problem. If this is not an option, the therapist may choose to work with the female partner alone, encouraging her to practice self-insertion, if this is acceptable to her.

CHAPTER 8

Importance of the Sexual Partner

When a couple likes each other and the partners are attracted to each other, most sexual problems can be worked out. Because a good partner relationship is so crucial to successful sex therapy, a therapist must focus on the relationship when treating sexual problems. Even with single individuals, it is important to focus on partner relations, so that a single person will be able to select a compatible partner when the time comes.

Principle Underlying Treatment

The principle to consider in couples treatment is that the severity of a couples nonsexual problems will determine the initial focus of therapy. If a couple has a positive attitude toward each other and are able to communicate effectively, sexual problems can be addressed immediately in therapy. If, on the other hand, there is considerable anger or distrust between a couple, or if the communication is problematic, these nonsexual issues must be addressed before sexual issues. In such cases, it is important to explain clearly to a couple that progress in overcoming sexual difficulties can best be assured if nonsexual issues are addressed first. In our experience, most couples readily understand and agree, even if they assumed the sexual issues would be the only focus.

Main Concept Conveyed to Client

The main concept to convey to clients is that blaming oneself or one's partner for a sexual problem is unproductive, and usually interferes with progress. Overcoming sexual problems is best achieved when a client and his or her partner work together.

Summary of Information

- Sexual attractions and the newness of a relationship often overshadow couples problems. The most common couples problems that interfere with sex are conflicts over control, poor communication, lack of common interests, and unresolved anger.

- Couples may harbor very negative feelings toward each other, yet still say they are in love. It is important to help a couple define what is meant by the word love, and help them understand their true feelings toward each other.

- A sexual partner's attitude toward sex and the degree of enthusiasm can greatly affect a person's sexual behavior. These partner issues are often overlooked, or thought to be unimportant, yet are crucial to a person's sexual responding.

- The ability to talk openly and honestly about sexual issues is important to solve sexual problems. Helping a couple establish effective communication skills, including quality time for communication, is a key therapeutic role. Chapter 8 in the Client Workbook contains a worksheet on positive communication skills.

Case Example

T: How are things going with you since the last time we met? It has been about two weeks.

C: Well, I thought everything was going okay. I suggested that we go to the movies, and at first she agreed, but then she got angry. We had a big fight and ended up not going. I still don't understand what the fight was about.

P: I agreed to go to the movies because it sounded like a good idea. But the more I thought about it, the more I got angry, because I have been asking for years to go out more and you never wanted to go (getting angry in tone). Now, we are in therapy and suddenly it seems like a good idea to you. You always ignore my wants and my feelings, and you do just what suits you. You never do anything for me.

T: (To client) Did you ask your wife the reason for her change in mind and the reason for her anger?

C: Yes. I said, "Why did you change your mind?" She said that I should know. I'm afraid to ask her much more because she starts crying or gets very angry. I feel that either way, I lose.

T: So what strategy do you use to solve problems between the two of you?

C: Basically, I just try to avold conflict as much as possible. I find that if I say nothing at all, the problem will go away.

T: (To partner) What are your thoughts when your husband is silent and doesn't respond to you?

P: I assume he doesn't care about me at all. He just ignores me and doesn't care what happens.

Clinical Comment

This brief exchange illustrates that this couple has considerable negative feelings toward each other and that basic communication skills are lacking. This couple does not solve problems, and consequently allows past problems and negative feelings to build. Terms like "always" and "never" are used freely, and thereby undermine positive efforts that are made. Also, the couple operates on second guessing each other, because silences and vague responses are common. This leads to misunderstandings and anger.

It would be extremely difficult, and probably a waste of therapy time, to attempt direct treatment of sexual problems before addressing the couple's faulty communication and lack of problem-solving skills. The pathway of treatment for this couple would best be structured to address the general communication and relationship problems first, and then the sexual problems (see Pathway Model, Figure 3.1). Although this couple originally presented for therapy because of lack of sexual desire, the initial assessment and treatment planning would identify the relationship as the first focus of treatment.

It should be noted, however, that some couples are unable to admit to or acknowledge their relationship problems, and may be very convincing to a therapist by avowing to the solidarity of their relationship. It is common that only after therapy is in progress, and the couple is challenged to deal with specific issues, that deep-seated problems emerge.

Atypical or Problematic Responses

A problematic response that many therapists may encounter is when one partner of a couple discloses that he or she is having a secret affair. In such situations, therapists must be careful not to impose their own morality. An evaluation of the affair, and the impact (if any) on the couple in therapy, must be made as objectively as possible. A determination of whether the person having the affair should disclose or end the affair must be made strictly from the couple's perspective.

Disclosure of an affair can be very destructive or very constructive depending on the strengths and weaknesses of each partner. In most cases, carrying on an affair is counterproductive to the therapeutic process. If the therapist judges the affair to be interfering or counterproductive to therapy, the person having the affair must be advised of this. It is then up to the therapist to help the client sort through their priorities and, in some cases, help the person end the affair. If the person chooses to continue the affair, the therapist is left with the difficult situation of sexual therapy that is not viable. Each therapist may have his or her own style of resolving this situation, but the important point is not to break confidentiality. If therapy is discontinued, do not leave the unsuspecting partner feeling that he or she is at fault for the discontinuation of therapy. At this point, it is possible to suggest an alternative referral, for one or both partners, to individual therapy.

CHAPTER 9

Working with a Partner to Master Your Sexual Problems

The Client Workbook, Chapter 8, emphasized the importance of a partner in treating sexual problems. Partners can be helpful or interfering, depending on their attitudes and skills. With single individuals, the *selection* of the "right" sexual partner is important. This chapter emphasizes several key ingredients to consider, once a client is working with a helpful partner.

Principle Underlying Treatment

There is one principle underlying treatment in this chapter. Even when couples have good communication and feel positive toward each other, improved sexual functioning is reached only when a couple establishes common sexual goals and has a shared responsibility for reaching those goals.

Main Concept Conveyed to Client

The main concept to convey to clients is that sex is most rewarding when favorable conditions exist for *both* partners. It is usual for one partner to be more desirous of sex than the other partner. When disparities in desire exist, couples should determine what is most comfortable for both. For example, one partner may say to his or her partner's sexual advance, "I don't feel like having intercourse, let's just snuggle." Such statements are intended to reach a comfortable level of intimacy without rejection.

Summary of Information

- Couples must be helped to establish their sexual goals. Should the couples' goals be to recapture a past enjoyable sexual relationship, establish a new more expanded sexual relationship, or adjust and modify their sexual relationship because of realistic changes in their lives, the therapist can help the partners discuss these options.

- Couples should again be reminded to set aside priority time for each other. This must be a commitment, not "catch as catch can." They should be encouraged to discuss favorable conditions under which sex can occur, and also identify unfavorable conditions.

- It is important that couples conceptualize their sexual problem as a shared problem. Blaming one another or viewing it as one person's problem is usually nonproductive. Even when it is clear that one partner brought the problem into the relationship, emphasize that the couple must work together in a step-by-step process to reach their goals. One partner can't just wait for the other partner "to get better." With such an attitude, the couple will miss opportunities to improve communication and move closer together.

Case Example

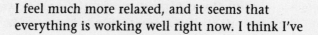

T: It has been about two weeks since we last met, and I want to review how you have been doing. We were focusing on two related areas. One area was your general stress level, and the other was your ability to focus on pleasure during sex. What has been your experience over the past two weeks?

C: I feel much more relaxed, and it seems that everything is working well right now. I think I've changed my attitude quite a bit. I now don't worry about everything, and I know there are lots of things I can't control.

T: (To partner) How do you feel things are going?

P: He definitely seems more relaxed. He can't tell when he is stressed out, but I can. I can read him like a book, and tell when he is nervous. He has trouble expressing his emotions. And when he is nervous, I become nervous.

C: Yeah, she does know me better than I know myself.

T: What has been your experience with sex during the past two weeks?

C: Everything worked well. I really got into it and we ended up having intercourse, although we didn't plan to. Again, my wife was very helpful. She told me it didn't matter if we had intercourse, and she really made me feel better.

P: He puts a lot of pressure on himself. I've always told him not to try so hard. Talking about it in therapy helped a lot.

T: Sex works best when you think about enjoying what you're doing rather than performing. Were you able to get lost in your thoughts during sex and just enjoy?

C: Because I wasn't even planning to have sex, I wasn't worried. Everything just seemed to work.

T: Were you actually able to have penetration and intercourse?

C: Yes.

T: I think this experience demonstrates to you how important your mental attitude is. Sex is like sleep. It is something you can't force, but you have to create the right conditions. Sleep works best when you feel sleepy and you're not worried about getting to sleep. If you try to force sleep when you aren't sleepy, or if you put pressure on yourself to go to sleep, it is usually interfered with. Sex is the same. It works best when you feel like having sex (when you are aroused), and when you just let it happen and don't try to force it.

C: That makes a lot of sense. I know I have been trying too hard.

T: (To partner) Because you are able to tell when your husband is stressed, you can help by letting him know, and suggesting at those times that it might be better just to hold each other.

P: I can do that. I think he will listen to me now.

Clinical Comment

The above example is a typical exchange. It illustrates a couple who communicate effectively and work well together. We have found that the analogy to sleep helps clients understand the negative impact on performance anxiety and trying too hard during sex.

Atypical or Problematic Responses

One common problem often encountered in sex therapy is limited quality time for sex. This occurs in married couples when they are both busy professionals or work different shifts. Also, this occurs in an individual without a steady partner when sexual opportunities are more random and unpredictable. When limited opportunities for sex exist, the tendency is to take advantage of an opportunity for sex even if one partner doesn't feel like it.

Such situations have to be thoroughly discussed with single individuals or couples to help reduce negative sexual experiences. A common statement by a client in such situations might be, "I know if we didn't try to have sex this weekend, it would be three weeks before we would have another opportunity. I tried having sex, although I didn't really want to."

Couples with such time constraints must be told that it is better to have a limited intimate experience that is pleasant, than to have a more full-scale sexual experience (usually meaning intercourse with orgasm) that is unrewarding. It is important for the therapist to help a couple communicate about their sexual feelings and accept, without negative repercussions, a more limited yet mutually pleasant and agreeable sexual encounter. Thus, a couple might forgo attempts at sexual intercourse in favor of holding, kissing, and caressing. Absolutely fantastic sex may only occur for a couple when they are able to get away together for a vacation.

CHAPTER 10

Mastering Your Sexual Problem

Chapter 10 of the Client Workbook helps clients put together all of the information they have learned thus far, to effectively deal with their sexual problem. At this point in the program, clients should have achieved an adequate sexual knowledge base, and should have established favorable conditions in their relationship.

Clients should also have achieved an understanding of the factors contributing to their sexual problem. This chapter helps clients further pinpoint the sources of their problem, and find possible solutions for overcoming it.

Principle Underlying Treatment

The main principle underlying treatment is that even with similar symptoms and presentation of problems, each case is unique and treatment strategies may be very different from client to client. Worksheet 10.1 in the Client Workbook allows the therapist to help the client address the unique issues that have led to his or her sexual problems (see Appendix A). Therapists should avoid jumping to conclusions just because a client's symptoms are similar to those of a previous client.

Main Concept Conveyed to Client

The main concept to convey to clients is that full treatment of sexual problems progresses in stages, and that within each stage, progress may move erratically. Couples may experience rapid progress on some issues and slow progress on others. Comprehensive treatment takes time, rarely goes smoothly, and often takes repetition and practice to achieve lasting changes. The therapist should summarize to the client what has been achieved so far, and what to expect in the next step.

Summary of Information

- Couples or individuals begin Chapter 10 by completing Worksheet 10.1 in the Client Workbook (see Appendix A). The worksheet helps pinpoint the various possible sources of a person's sexual problem: personal, interpersonal, and medical. Each item on the worksheet corresponds to a "source" presented in the chapter. Clients may find general information pertaining to each item they have checked "yes," and a suggested treatment strategy. The general information and specific suggestions for each source item will help clients understand how the source has contributed to their sexual problem, and how they can begin to overcome the problem. By addressing all items marked "yes," the therapist guides the client through a comprehensive treatment program.

- In addition to addressing the personal sources of a sexual problem, there is often a need to address the specific nature of the sexual problem itself. For example, a woman may have complained of low sexual arousal. When she reviews Worksheet 10.1, she may check off Items 1 and 4 under personal sources, Item 3 under interpersonal sources, and Item 2 under medical sources. The general information and specific suggestions should be addressed for each of these items. After addressing each item, she should turn to the specific guidelines in her workbook for treating low sexual arousal. Under this section, she will be guided through sensate focus. The combination of addressing all items checked "yes" as sources of sexual problems, and responding to the treatment suggestions, will complete her treatment program.

Treatment Guidelines

The treatment guidelines for specific problem areas are outlined below
for therapists, whether or not your clients are using the *Enhancing
Sexuality* Client Workbook. Comprehensive treatment, of course, depends
on your assessment. It should identify all the relevant factors contributing
to your client's sexual problem. The most common treatment approach
for each problem area will follow. In any problem area, there may
be additional appropriate treatment strategies depending on the nuances
of your client's problem.

Erection and Arousal Problems

The therapeutic strategy of sensate focus is most commonly used
for erection problems in men and arousal problems in women (Masters
& Johnson, 1966). The therapist's role is to help clients understand why
this is a worthwhile approach to overcoming sexual problems. Some
clients will say that they tried this approach, but it did not work. In most
cases, however, the client assumes that sexual intercourse will proceed
if everything is functioning. The therapist must point out that sensate
focus is a focus on sensations, not function. The reason that previous
attempts might not have worked may be because the client allowed
function to be the ultimate goal, even if this was not originally intended.
Sensate focus works best when a couple agrees to a prescribed scenario
and sticks to it.

The therapist should explain to the client that sex works best when
an individual is only thinking about sensations, and not what each
partner wants to do to the other partner. Although these are normal,
healthy, sexual thoughts about performance, they may interfere with
function. Sensate focus, it should be explained, is a strategy to help
get a person back to focusing on sensation. It is a means to an end,
and not the end itself or description of how sex "will be" for a couple.

The therapist should talk in detail to each couple using the sensate focus
strategy, including at what point in a continuum of behaviors the couple
should start; how often and where a couple should practice; how long
each session should last (give a range of time from 15 to 30 minutes);
what the goals of the sessions are; and how each session should
be initiated as well as who is responsible for initiating. Explain to clients
that the goal of sensate focus is not sexual arousal, although many find
the process arousing, but to enjoy the sensations without having to worry
about function. In addition, the sensate focus procedure usually helps

couples communicate their sexual needs, because they are encouraged to give positive feedback to each other about what felt good.

The sensate focus strategy begins by explaining to the client or couple that sexual problems are often maintained by focusing too much on performance. What is needed is a focus on sensations or pleasure. The focus on sensations is necessary to break the negative cycle of focusing on performance. To break this cycle, the couple must set aside specific relaxed times when pleasure can be explored without any expectations for performance. Key ingredients for successful sensate focus by a couple usually include an agreed prohibition on intercourse, no matter what degree of arousal occurs; a conceptualization of sex as a menu of behaviors to choose from, not as something that must be "completed" with intercourse; and sex play, erotic massage, and affection as positive sexual exchanges, and not as "teasing" or "misleading" in a negative, hurtful sense. The couple should provide the therapist with descriptions of their practice. The therapist should offer suggestions on how to work through specific problems, and explain what the next steps are for the couple. Such suggestions might include how to break down specific behaviors into simpler stops, and when to include intercourse in the sensate focus sessions.

Quick Ejaculation

The strategy most helpful to men experiencing premature ejaculation is a combination of providing accurate and realistic information about men's ejaculation, and helping a man and his partner focus on pleasure rather than performance. Most men ejaculate within 2 to 8 minutes of penetration. Age and time since last ejaculation will affect speed of ejaculation to some degree. Focus on pleasure during intercourse means to reinforce that the ejaculation should be enjoyed and not cursed, and that after ejaculation, intercourse should continue to prolong pleasure, rather than abruptly stopping (as is common) upon ejaculation.

Difficulty Achieving Orgasm

The most common treatment strategy used for treating orgasmic problems in men and women is outlined in detail on page 61. The most important ingredients in treatment include providing clients with a realistic understanding of the orgasmic experience and the normal individual variations. It is also important to explore options with clients that will provide the maximum erotic stimulation in a conducive environment, possibly using vibratory stimulation or a lubricant. Therapists are again reminded to be cautious not to focus on performance.

Difficulty with Pain and Penetration

Sexual pain and penetration problems must be referred to a physician to screen out possible medical contributions. Once medical factors have been evaluated and dismissed, or treated, psychological treatment can begin. The most useful strategy is to encourage a gradual, step-by-step approach to sexual insertion. Teaching relaxation, and breaking sexual approach behaviors into discrete, manageable steps, are helpful treatment ingredients. It is important for the therapist to explore with the client the point in sexual activity where comfort ends and discomfort begins. That is the point at which a client starts practice.

Practice may or may not include a partner, depending on availability of a partner and the comfort level of the client. Practice without a partner often includes looking at and touching one's genitals. For women, practice may include gradual insertion of one's finger. Each step a client will practice should be discussed thoroughly in therapy, and practiced by the client in a private, relaxed setting.

Practice with a partner will usually include outlining for couples the specific steps (e.g., touching outside a vagina with finger, but no insertion) to be practiced during a week, and emphasizing that the client can stop a practice trial at any time to reduce anxiety. However, trials should be repeated until a step is accomplished with comfort. An entire hierarchy of sexual approach behaviors should be established at the beginning as a guideline for therapy goals.

Low Sex Drive

The expression by a client of a sexual desire problem is often confusing. It is important for the therapist to differentiate sexual desire (horniness) from worry about sex. In true sexual desire disorders, there is an absence of horniness and sexual fantasies. It is also important for the therapist to determine if there ever was a time that the client felt desire, or if there are currently conditions under which a client feels desire. Clients with a sexual profile in which they never felt sexual desire are extremely difficult to treat. On the other hand, clients who are able to identify past times or current conditions in which sexual desire has been, or is present, are more easily treated. After ruling out medical conditions or specific medications that can affect desire, therapy usually proceeds with identifying currently inhibiting personal or interpersonal factors.

General worry, anxiety, or depression can affect sexual desire. Treating these conditions often restores sexual desire. In some cases, the suggested use of erotic stimulation (videos, books, magazines, or movies) may have a positive effect on sexual desire. This topic has to be approached cautiously, as does the topic of vibrators, to ensure that individuals or couples are not offended.

Case Example

T: How do each of you feel about working more directly on sexual relations? So far, you have worked on improving communication and structuring your time together. This seems to have improved your readiness to address sexual problems.

C: I think the biggest step has been that we don't blame each other anymore. Neither of us had any sexual experience before marriage, and we just expected that everything would work well once we were married.

P: I was never aware of how my upbringing made me so negative about sex. I thought that once I got married, I would feel differently. When my husband approached me for sex on our wedding night, I thought he was an animal. I couldn't believe his change when I couldn't go through with sex. He became angry, and I wondered if I should have gotten married.

C: I thought that she was angry at me for some reason and was trying to punish me. We never discussed it, and each of us was angry.

T: How do you look at that experience now?

C: I tend to judge people quickly without finding out all of the facts. I simply made some assumptions and operated on these assumptions without checking with my wife.

P: I was intimidated by his anger and I just endured sex, but hated it. Now I can see that it is something to enjoy.

T: The next step in our program is to gradually approach sex in a comfortable way, without pressure. It is very important that sex occurs at times that are agreeable to both of you. If there is any discomfort or stress, it is okay to stop. Each of you has to agree to this, and not respond with anger or disappointment. Remember, think of sex as a pleasurable activity that may include a variety of behaviors. You may pick and choose what you want to do, and you can stop at any time. Many couples have the idea that, once they start something, they must finish it. This usually means sexual intercourse. This attitude often leads to total avoidance of sex. A person may feel like hugging and kissing, but not want to have intercourse. By agreeing to the procedure I am proposing, you should feel less pressure and may increase the overall amount of physical contact. You will also guarantee that when sexual intercourse does occur, it is mutually desired.

P: I still feel that I would be disappointing my husband if I asked him to stop.

C: I may be disappointed, but it really is okay. I understand things better now, so I'm not going to be a jerk like before.

Clinical Comment

This is a typical exchange between a couple who have spent the initial stages of therapy working on improving communication. If therapy had initially focused on their sexual relationship, without first laying the appropriate foundation, it would have failed. The knowledge and understanding gained from a discussion of each person's sexual development helped remove blame. Improving communication skills is necessary to diffuse the anger present from early sexual conflicts and ongoing struggles over control issues.

Atypical or Problematic Responses

Sometimes, after initial successful progress, couples will run into roadblocks or experience a setback, and readily return to former destructive patterns. Initial success may have led to a false sense of security, or expectations that were too high. We have often seen couples who have worked on problems and shown some success. Then they go away on vacation and experience great sex. A return home to face day-to-day stresses may have subsequently interfered with sex, and the couple feels they have failed and are "back to square one." In such cases, it is important for the therapist to remind the couple of their previous progress, and to assure them that all is not lost. A review of the circumstances related to success and failure will help identify elements that contributed to such a varied experience. This can be used therapeutically to reinforce the need for reviewing important principles. This will also set the stage for understanding relapse prevention.

CHAPTER 11

Continuing Progress
and Avoiding Roadblocks

Individuals and couples sometimes feel an increase in their stress when they begin to work directly on sexual issues. It is important that clients and therapists recognize and address stalled progress as soon as it occurs.

Principle Underlying Treatment

Therapists can help deal with stalling in therapy more effectively if it is identified as a possibility and discussed at the beginning of therapy. The main principle to keep in mind is that sexual dysfunction is an extremely upsetting experience, and treatment deserves the utmost sensitivity to each client's pain. It is difficult for most clients to admit they have a sexual problem, and come to therapy to discuss and work on overcoming it. Stalling is not unusual, and the therapist must create a trusting environment in which clients feel free to talk about the occurrence of stalling.

Main Concept Conveyed to Client

The main concept conveyed to clients is that stalled progress is not a random event. It is important to clearly identify why progress has stalled and work through that issue.

Summary of Information

■ Guidelines are given to help clients identify avoidance and take corrective steps. Clients are made sensitive to the distinction between avoidance and realistic interference with progress. Sexual partners should review problems and take corrective steps to allow progress to continue.

■ Review *commitment* to work on the sex problem. The therapist should help couples raise the issue of whether or not they are truly committed to working on their sexual problem. Commitment means to prioritize therapy and practice sessions so that nothing other than emergencies interferes with these efforts. A couple should reaffirm their commitment in the therapy session.

■ Review the *comfort* that each partner has with the therapy plan. The therapist should review the therapy plan and ask each partner if they are completely comfortable with the plan. Help identify any changes or new perspectives that may have resulted from therapy or practice that altered the comfort level.

■ Review each partner's *expectations* about the therapy strategy. Expectations may have changed or been misunderstood, and it is worthwhile to ensure that both partners' expectations for therapy and practice are understood and accepted.

■ Review the final *goals* of therapy to ensure that each agrees. Often, when therapy works in stages, clients forget that the stages or steps are necessary to achieve the final goals. A review of the final goals and how these goals can be achieved by the therapy strategy is helpful.

■ If progress continues to stall, a couple or individual client may have to set different goals. In some cases, sexual dysfunction may serve a purpose that, in some way, satisfies a client's need. This possibility should be explored by the therapist. Gentle probing is suggested here, because the client may or may not be aware of the secondary gain provided by the sexual dysfunction.

Case Example

T: It has been two weeks since we last met. How have things gone for you?

C: Well, we had my mother visit us, and my car battery went dead, and it just seems like we were too busy to do anything.

P: We were awfully busy, and I had to shop and cook because his mother was visiting. It is always very stressful when she visits. She is very critical and everything has to be just right.

T: (To client) How long was your mother's visit?

C: For two days, but it was right on the weekend.

T: Did you discuss practicing the sexual program at some other time?

C: No, we didn't. I think we both got so focused on my mother that we forgot about it.

P: I didn't forget about it, but I felt it was his responsibility to make plans to practice. He always leaves everything up to me. Besides he puts his mother's wishes ahead of mine.

T: (To client) Is there a lot of conflict related to your mother?

P: Shortly after we got married, my husband told me that his mother thought he married beneath himself. He insisted that he loved me, but I always wondered if he really did.

C: I told you I loved you. What more could
I say? Just because I do things for my mother
doesn't mean I don't love you.

Clinical Comment

This is an example of a situation in which stalling led to a discussion
that uncovered a long-standing, unresolved issue. This couple
had never thoroughly dealt with the issue of the husband's mother
or how it affected his partner. Before further progress on the sexual issue
(low desire on the part of the partner) could be expected, the couple
had to work through their feelings.

It is helpful if, at the end of each therapy session, the therapist asks
the client(s) whether any events will be coming up before the next
therapy session that will affect practice in any way. Although not
all interfering situations can be anticipated, many can be effectively dealt
with ahead of time.

Atypical or Problematic Responses

We have dealt with clients who, for one reason or another, have had long
periods of time in which their usual sexual partner was not available.
Pregnancy and subsequent birth of a child, tours of duty in the service,
and long-term business commitments out of the country, have all been
situations we have encountered that have interrupted ongoing therapy.
In such cases, we have outlined progress that has been achieved
by the couple, and issues that remain to be dealt with. Whenever possible,
we have encouraged reviewing appropriate reading material and, in some
cases, worked on individual issues to bridge the gap. Sessions with
the available partner alone have sometimes also been helpful to bridge
the gap, until a time that the couple could resume therapy together.

CHAPTER 12

Relapse Prevention

At this point, clients have satisfactorily completed the *Enhancing Sexuality* program, and therapy is endlng. This chapter gives relapse prevention guidelines so couples can maintain therapy gains.

Principles Underlying Treatment

Treatment gains can easily erode without proper planning. Relapse prevention can successfully be achieved by discussing possible future problems and thoroughly rehearsing effective responses. Reminding clients of all their resources, and reviewing their gains from the beginning of therapy is also helpful.

Main Concept Conveyed to Client

The main concept conveyed to clients is that they have the tools and ability to effectively deal with their sexual problems. Identifying any early warning signs, talking openly with their sexual partner, rereading helpful material, and seeking booster therapy sessions are all within their power.

Summary of Information

- Suggestions are given to help clients identify and measure when their treatment gains have slipped back. Four areas are suggested as a barometer of sexual satisfaction. They are how often affection is shown to a partner, how often sexual contacts are made with a partner, how comfortable a client is at approaching sex, and whether or not sexual experiences are of a quality nature.

- There are no set standards for the above four areas. Rather, subjective scaling is suggested that should be established by each client at the end of therapy.

- Maintaining gains takes vigilance and work. Clients are encouraged to periodically check on the quality of their sexual relationship, especially after important life changes.

Case Example

T: How do you feel about your sexual relationship at this time?

C: I really feel satisfied with the way everything has gone. In fact, on our ride over here, my husband asked me what we were going to talk about. We both felt that we no longer had problems.

P: I agree. We are both very happy. I can't believe how much we have changed.

T: I'm pleased that you both feel that way, and I think we should discuss how to make sure everything stays on track. How would each of you identify if you were slipping back into some of your old patterns?

C: I think the first thing I would notice would be if my husband started withdrawing more, and doing what he used to, like watching TV and not talking to me.

P: I think I would notice if my wife started nagging me more.

T: Certainly, each of you will watch TV and nag at each other in the future, so let's talk about how to more precisely tell if there is a change back to the old ways. Also, we should talk about what to do if you do feel progress has slipped back. (To client) What do you mean by the comment about your husband watching too much TV, and what would you do if you thought that?

C: Before we started therapy, he would watch TV from the time he came home from work until he went to bed. As he said previously, it was his way to unwind from work. Since we have been in therapy, he only watches the news and other programs once in a while. The biggest change is that the TV is not on when we are eating, so we talk a lot more. I think if he started watching TV during dinner, I would say something. I would remind him that we have a different agreement now.

T: (To partner) How would you respond to that approach?

P: That would be fine, as long as she said it the way she just did. In the past, it sounded like nagging.

Clinical Comment

It is important for the therapist to help the couple work with meaningful and agreeable criteria. The criteria should be set up as mutual consent between two adults who are working at the same goal. The therapist must be sure that criteria do not come across as blame or faultfinding. We are all subject to slip into old patterns, and it is helpful if each partner reminds the other to stay on track.

Atypical or Problematic Responses

Couples sometimes become so dependent on therapy that there is great insecurity in therapy termination. There is a sense in these couples that all progress will reverse as soon as therapy stops. In such cases, the termination is set up in gradual steps of fading out, with increasing time between sessions. Also, reviewing the progress and resources, and setting up at least one distant therapy session (4 to 6 months later), is often enough reassurance for couples to terminate with confidence.

APPENDIX A

Common Causes or Sources of Sex Problems

Personal Sources:

1. When you were a child or teenager, did messages about sex or your body make you upset or uneasy? ☐ Yes ☐ No

2. As a child or teenager, did you receive correct information about sex? ☐ Yes ☐ No

3. As a child or teenager, were you a victim of sexual abuse or did you know of friends or family who were? ☐ Yes ☐ No

4. As an adult, have you ever had an experience with sex that made you feel upset or ashamed? ☐ Yes ☐ No

5. Do you have general anger toward or fear of the opposite sex? ☐ Yes ☐ No

6. Do you now have a personal problem that is not related to sex, such as low self-esteem, worry, depression, trauma, or fear? ☐ Yes ☐ No

7. When you have an opportunity for sex, is it in a private, comfortable place? ☐ Yes ☐ No

8. Do you feel confused about your sexual direction? ☐ Yes ☐ No

Interpersonal Sources:

1. Is your sex partner tense or uneasy about sex or does he or she seem uninterested? □ Yes □ No

2. Does your partner have his or her own sex problems? □ Yes □ No

3. Is it hard for you to talk with your sex partner? □ Yes □ No

4. Do you feel tension or anger toward your sex partner? □ Yes □ No

5. Do you lack physical attraction toward your partner? □ Yes □ No

6. Do you have a strong physical attraction toward someone other than your partner? □ Yes □ No

Medical Sources:

1. Are you now using or abusing alcohol or other drugs? □ Yes □ No

2. Are you taking a drug to treat a mental problem, high blood pressure, ulcers, or seizures? □ Yes □ No

3. Do you have diabetes, heart disease, nerve disease, or spinal cord injury? □ Yes □ No

4. Do you have a health condition that causes you to feel self-conscious or embarrassed? Do you have one that causes pain, fatigue, or nausea? □ Yes □ No

5. If you are male, do you *not* have erections at any time? That is, when you are with a partner, when you masturbate, or at night when you wake up? □ Yes □ No

References

Abrahamson, D. J., Barlow, D. H., & Abrahamson, L. S. (1989). Differential effects of performance demand and distraction on sexually functional and dysfunctional males. *Journal of Abnormal Psychology, 98*(3), 241–247.

Abrahamson, D. J., Barlow, D. H., Beck, J. G., Sakheim, D. K., & Kelly, J. P. (1985). The effects of attentional focus and partner responsiveness on sexual responding: Replication and extension. *Archives of Sexual Behavior, 14*(4), 361–371.

Abrahamson, D. J., Barlow, D. H., Sakheim, D. K., Beck, J. G., & Athanasiou, R. (1985). Effects of distraction on sexual responding in functional and dysfunctional men. *Behavior Therapy, 16,* 503–515.

American Psychiatric Association. (1994). *Diagnostic and statistical manual of mental disorders* (4th ed.). Washington, DC: Author.

Balko, A., Malhotra, C. M., Wincze, J. P., Susset, J. G., & Bansal, S., Carney, W. I., & Hopkins, R. W. (1986). Deep penile vein arterialization for arterial and venous impotence. *Archives of Surgery, 121*(7), 774–777.

Barlow, D. H. (1972). [Review of the book Homosexual behaviour: Therapy and assessment]. *Behavior Therapy, 3,* 479–481.

Barlow, D. H. (1973). Increasing heterosexual responsiveness in the treatment of sexual deviation: A review of the clinical and experimental evidence. *Behavior Therapy, 4,* 655–671.

Barlow, D. H. (1977a). Assessment of sexual behavior. In A. R. Ciminero, K. S. Calhoun, & H. E. Adams (Eds.), *Handbook of behavioral assessment* (pp. 461–508). New York: John Wiley & Sons.

Barlow, D. H. (1977b). Behavioral assessment in clinical settings: Developing issues. In J. D. Cone & R. P. Hawkins (Eds.), *Behavioral assessment: New directions in clinical psychology* (pp. 283–307). New York: Brunner-Mazel.

Barlow, D. H. (1986). The causes of sexual dysfunction: The role of anxiety and cognitive interference. *Journal of Consulting and Clinical Psychology, 54*(2), 140–148.

Barlow, D. H., Abel, G. G., Blanchard, E. B., Bristow, A. R., & Young, L. D. (1977). A heterosocial skills behavior checklist for males. *Behavior Therapy, 8,* 229–239.

Barlow, D. H., Becker, R., Leitenberg, H., & Agras, W. S. (1970). A mechanical strain gauge for recording penile circumference change. *Journal of Applied Behavior Analysis, 3*(1), 73–76.

Barlow, D. H., Sakheim, D. K., & Beck, J. G. (1983). Anxiety increases sexual arousal. *Journal of Abnormal Psychology, 92*(1), 49–54.

Beck, J. G., & Barlow, D. H. (1984a). Current conceptualizations of sexual dysfunction: A review and an alternative perspective. *Clinical Psychology Review, 4,* 363–378.

Beck J. G., & Barlow, D. H. (1984b). Unraveling the nature of sex roles. In E. A. Blechman (Ed.), *Behavior modification with women* (pp. 34–59). New York: Guilford Press.

Beck, J. G., & Barlow, D. H. (1986a). The effects of anxiety and attentional focus on sexual responding: I. Physiological patterns in erectile dysfunction. *Behaviour Research and Therapy, 24*(1), 9–17.

Beck, J. G., & Barlow, D. H. (1986b). The effects of anxiety and attentional focus on sexual responding: II. Cognitive and affective patterns in erectile dysfunction. *Behaviour Research and Therapy, 24*(1), 19–26.

Beck, J. G., Barlow, D. H., & Sakheim, D. K. (1983a). Abdominal temperature changes during male sexual arousal. *Psychophysiology, 20*(6), 715–717.

Beck, J. G., Barlow, D. H., & Sakheim, D. K. (1983b). The effects of attentional focus and partner arousal on sexual responding in functional and dysfunctional men. *Behaviour Research and Therapy, 21*(1), 1–8.

Beck, J. G., Barlow, D. H., Sakheim, D. K., & Abrahamson, D. J. (1987). Shock threat and sexual arousal. The role of selective attention, thought content, and affective states. *Psychophysiology, 24*(2), 165–172.

Beck, J. G., Sakheim, D. K., & Barlow, D. H. (1983). Operating characteristics of the vaginal photoplethysmograph: Some implications for its use. *Archives of Sexual Behavior, 12*(1), 43–58.

Bruce, T. J., & Barlow, D. H. (1990). The nature and role of performance anxiety in sexual dysfunction. In H. Leitenberg (Ed.), *Handbook of social and evaluation anxiety*. New York: Plenum Press.

Caird, W. K., & Wincze, J. P. (1974). Videotaped desensitization of frigidity. *Journal of Behavior Therapy and Experimental Psychiatry, 5,* 175–178.

Caird, W. K., & Wincze, J. P. (1977). *Sex therapy: A behavioral approach.* Hagerstown, MD: Harper & Row.

Carey, M. P., Wincze, J. P., & Meisler, A. W. (1993). Sexual dysfunction: Male erectile disorder. In D. H. Barlow (Ed.) *Clinical handbook of psychological disorders. A step-by-step treatment manual* (2nd ed., pp. 442–480). New York: Guilford Press.

Cranston-Cuebas, M. A., & Barlow, D. H. (1990). Cognitive and affective contributions to sexual functioning. *Annual Review of Sex Research, 1,* 119–161.

Cranston-Cuebas, M. A., Barlow, D. H., Mitchell, W., & Athanasiou, R. (1993). Differential effects of misattribution manipulation on sexually functional and dysfunctional men. *Journal of Abnormal Psychology, 102*(4), 525–533.

Freund, K., Langevin, R., & Barlow, D. H. (1974). Comparison of two penile measures of erotic arousal. *Behaviour Research and Therapy, 12*(4), 355–359.

Hoon, E. F., Hoon, P. W., & Wincze, J. P. (1976). An inventory for the measurement of female sexual arousability: The SAI. *Archives of Sexual Behavior, 5*(4), 269–274.

Hoon, E. F., Krop, H. D., & Wincze, J. P. (1983). Sexuality. In E. A. Blechman (Ed.), *Behavior modification with women* (pp. 113–142). New York: Guilford Press.

Hoon, P. W., Wincze, J. P., & Hoon, E. F. (1976). Physiological assessment of sexual arousal in women. *Psychophysiology, 13*(3), 196–204.

Hoon, P. W., Wincze, J. P., & Hoon, E. F. (1977). The effects of biofeedback and cognitive mediation upon vaginal blood volume. *Behavior Therapy, 8,* 694–702.

Jones, J. C., & Barlow, D. H. (1990). Self-reported frequency of sexual urges, fantasies, and masturbatory fantasies in heterosexual males and females. *Archives of Sexual Behavior, 19*(3), 269–279.

Lange, J. D., Brown, W. A., Wincze, J. P., & Zwick, W. (1980). Serum testosterone concentration and penile tumescence changes in men. *Hormones and Behavior, 14*(3), 267–270.

Lange, J. D., Wincze, J. P., Zwick, W., Feldman, S., & Hughes, K. (1981). Effects of demand for performance, self-monitoring of arousal, and increased sympathetic nervous system activity on the male erectile response. *Archives of Sexual Behavior, 10*(5), 443–464.

Malhotra, C. M., Balko, A., Wincze, J. P., Bansal, S., & Susset, J. G. (1986). Cavernosography in conjunction with artificial erection by saline infusion for evaluation of venous leakage in impotent men. *Radiology, 161*(3), 799–802.

Masters, W. H., & Johnson, V. E. (1966). *Human sexual response.* Boston: Little Brown.

Masters, W. H., Johnson, V. E., & Kolodny, R. C. (1992). *Human sexuality.* New York: Harper Collins Publishers.

Sakheim, D. K., Barlow, D. H., Beck, J. G., & Abrahamson, D. J. (1984). The effect of an increased awareness of erectile cues on sexual arousal. *Behavior Research and Therapy, 22*(2), 151–158.

Steinman, D. L., Wincze, J. P., Sakheim, D. K., Barlow, D. H., & Mavissakalian, M. (1981). A comparison of male and female patterns of sexual arousal. *Archives of Sexual Behavior, 10*(6), 529–547.

Turner, J. S., & Rubinson, L. (1993). *Contemporary human sexuality.* Englewood Cliffs, NJ: Prentice Hall.

Wincze, J. P. (1993). [Review of the book Erectile disorders: An integration of medical and psychological information]. *Contemporary Psychology, 38*(4), 390–391.

Wincze, J. P. (1995). Marital discord and sexual dysfunction associated with a male partner's "sexual addiction". In R. C. Rosen and S. R. Leiblum (Eds.), *Case studies in sex therapy,* (pp. 380–392). New York: Guilford Press.

Wincze, J. P., Albert, A., & Bansal, S. (1993). Sexual arousal in diabetic females: Physiological and self-report measures. *Archives of Sexual Behavior, 22*(6), 587–601.

Wincze, J. P., Bansal, S., Malhotra, C., Balko, A., Susset, J. G., & Malamud, M. (1987). The use of psychophysiological techniques in the assessment of male sexual dysfunction (in) *Proceedings of the American Cancer Society's Workshop on Psychosexual and Reproductive Issues of Cancer Clients.*

Wincze, J. P., Bansal, S., Malhotra, C., Balko, A., Susset, J. G., & Malamud, M. (1988). A comparison of nocturnal penile tumescence and penile response to erotic stimulation during waking states in comprehensively diagnosed groups of males experiencing erectile difficulties. *Archives of Sexual Behavior, 17*(4), 333–348.

Wincze, J. P., & Barlow, D. H. (1997). *Enhancing Sexuality: A problem-solving approach client workbook.* San Antonio, TX: The Psychological Corporation.

Wincze, J. P., & Caird, W. K. (1976). The effects of systematic desensitization and video desensitization in the treatment of essential sexual dysfunction in women. *Behavior Therapy, 7,* 335–342.

Wincze, J. P., & Carey, M. P. (1991). *Sexual dysfunction: A guide for assessment and treatment.* New York: Guilford Press.

Wincze, J. P., Hoon, E. F., & Hoon, P. W. (1976). Physiological responsivity of normal and sexually dysfunctional women during erotic stimulus exposure. *Journal of Psychomatic Research, 20*(5), 445–451.

Wincze, J. P., Hoon, P. W., & Hoon, E. F. (1977). Sexual arousal in women: A comparison of cognitive and physiological responses by continuous measurement. *Archives of Sexual Behavior, 6*(2), 121–133.

Wincze, J. P., Hoon, E. F., & Hoon, P. W. (1978). Multiple measure analysis of women experiencing low sexual arousal. *Behavior Research and Therapy, 16*(1), 43–49.

Wincze, J. P., Venditti, E., Barlow, D. H., & Mavissakalian, M. (1980). The effects of a subjective monitoring task on the physiological measure of genital response to erotic stimulation. *Archives of Sexual Behavior, 9*(6), 533–545.

Wolchick, S. A., Beggs, V. E., Wincze, J. P., Sakheim, D. K., Barlow, D. H., & Mavissakalian, M. (1980). The effect of emotional arousal on subsequent sexual arousal in men. *Journal of Abnormal Psychology, 89*(4), 595–598.

For information on Graywind Publications or TherapyWorks products, please contact The Psychological Corporation at **1-800-228-0752 (TDD 1-800-723-1318).**